ABUNDANT TRUTH INTERNATIONAL MINISTRIES

Mikhtam Music Worship Series

Mikhtam Music Presents...

Come Let Us Worship

*

Appreciating the Call to Worship

R.L. Evans
"Mikhtam Maestro"

Mikhtam Music Presents...
Come Let Us Worship
Appreciating the Call to Worship

All Rights Reserved. Copyright © 2025 R.L. Evans

No part of this book may be reproduced or transmitted in any form or by any means, graphic, electronic, or mechanical, including photocopying, recording, taping or by any information storage or retrieval system, without the permission in writing from the publisher.

Cover Designs by Abundant Truth Publishing

Abundant Truth Publishing
an imprint of Abundant Truth International Ministries

For information address:
Abundant Truth International
P.O. Box 126
Camden, NC 27921

ISBN 13: 978-1-60141-659-9

Printed in the United States of America

Unless otherwise indicated, all of the scripture quotations are taken from the *Authorized King James Version* of the Bible. Scripture quotations marked with NIV are taken from the *New International Version* of the Bible. Scripture quotations marked with NASV are taken from the *New American Standard Version* of the Bible. Scripture quotations marked with Amplified are taken from the *Amplified Bible*.

Table of Contents

Preface

Introduction

Section 1 – I and the Lad will go Yonder and Worship   1

Worship is Sacrifice   5
Worship is Subsistence   11
Worship is Selfless   13

Section 2 – O Come, Let Us Worship and Bow Down   17

Bowing of the Head   22
Bowing at the Waist   24
Bending of the Knee(s)   27
Prostrating the Body   29

Table of Contents *(cont.)*

Section 3 – Worship In Action	35
Bow/Prostate to His Standards for Living	*37*
Swim in (Live in) His Presence	*39*
Serve the Lord in Ministry and Good Works	*40*
Glossary of Terms	47
Bibliography	51

Preface

I am grateful to the Lord for all He has done in my life. His wonderful works are seen daily not only in my life, but also in the life of all those that call upon His name. Because of His goodness, believers should be inspired to worship and praise His name.

I have written this book to challenge and encourage others to worship the Lord in spirit and in truth.

R.L. Evans

Introduction

What is worship? What is praise and adoration? These questions remain on the frontlines of discussion in Christianity. How does one express worship, praise, and adoration in the Christian Church?

To answer these questions in depth, the Mikhtam Music Worship Series was developed. In this series, we will define worship and how it is to be expressed in the New Testament worship experience.

In this publication:

What is worship? What is praise and adoration? These questions remain on the frontlines of discussion in Christianity. How does one express worship, praise, and adoration in the Christian Church? Does worship consist of silence in the sanctuary? Or, is worship not worship until someone sings or lifts the hands?

In the pages of the Bible, various forms of worship are presented. Silent and vocal worship are described, as well as exuberant and clamorous forms of worship. So, which is the proper way to worship the Lord?

From the scriptures, we learn that God expects to be worshipped in many ways. There is not a set worship style that is deemed mandatory. However, one criterion does exist.

> *God is a Spirit: and they that worship him must worship him in spirit and in truth. (John 4:24)*

God requires His worship to be offered in spirit, which could also be translated sincerity. True worship begins with a sincere heart. Alongside sincerity, truth has to be incorporated into God's worship. Worship that is not founded upon the truth of God is vain and leads men into deception.

When there is an understanding of God, Christ, and His plan for man, worship, praise, and adoration will become more than an external exercise of singing, lifting up hands, and jubilation. Worship, praise, and adoration will become the driving force in the life of the Christian.

Worship, praise, and adoration is not designed for man, but it is for the Lord. All of God's creation is endued with the responsibility and ability to worship, praise, and glorify the Lord.

> *Let the heavens rejoice, and let the earth be glad; let the sea roar, and the fullness thereof. Let the field be joyful, and all that is therein: then shall all the trees of the wood rejoice before the Lord. (Psalms 96:11-13a)*

If all of creation praises Him, those that He has given dominion over creation have the command to worship and praise His holiness. Thus, man was created to worship, praise, and glorify Him.

This people have I formed for myself; they shall show forth my praise. (Isaiah 43:21)

The prophet declared that God called Israel unto Himself that they may praise Him. The nation existed to praise God. Since Christians become God's chosen through Jesus Christ, like Israel, they receive the same description.

But ye are a chosen generation, a royal priesthood, an holy nation, a peculiar people; that ye should show forth the praises of him who hath called you out of darkness into his marvelous light. (I Peter 2:9)

The Christian's worship, praise, and adoration of God transcend the gathering together in churches. It extends into everyday life. The call to worship, praise, and adoration is not only for religious ceremonies and for assemblies, but it also has to characterize the believer's lifestyle and existence.

In the first book of this series, we will discuss the various dimensions of worship. Through the examination of biblical and religious terminology, a proper

Appreciation of the believer's call to worship is established.****

Come, Let Us Worship [*Appreciating the Call to Worship*]

-Section 1-

I and the Lad will go Yonder and Worship
-*Genesis 22:5*

Come, Let Us Worship
[Appreciating the Call to Worship]

Come, Let Us Worship
[Appreciating the Call to Worship]

The true essence of worship does not begin with religious adulations bestowed upon God. It begins with the lifestyle of those who serve Him. To understand worship, we have to look at its usage in the scriptures.

In the King James Version of the Bible, the word *worship* appears for the first time in Genesis 22.

It was not used in religious service or in association with praying, singing, or the lifting of hands. Worship was used to describe an upcoming sacrifice.

Come, Let Us Worship
[Appreciating the Call to Worship]

And Abraham said unto his young men, Abide ye here with the ass; and I and the lad will go yonder and worship, and come again to you. (Genesis 22:5)

The Lord spoke to Abraham and commanded him to sacrifice his son Isaac. This was simply a test of Abraham's faith. When the time came for Abraham and Isaac to ascend to the place of sacrifice, Abraham makes a profound statement.

He declares that the potential sacrifice (of his son) was worship. This brings us to

Come, Let Us Worship [*Appreciating the Call to Worship*]

the first component of worship.

Worship is Sacrifice

The worship of God finds its roots in sacrifice. Abraham was willing to sacrifice someone that was dear to him in order to worship.

And he said, Take now thy son, thine only son Isaac, whom thou lovest, and get thee into the land of Moriah; and offer him there for a burnt offering upon one of the mountains which I will tell thee of. (Genesis 22:2)

Come, Let Us Worship [*Appreciating the Call to Worship*]

Before we can enter into God's presence fully via worship, we have to be willing to give up everything first. Abraham was prepared to sacrifice what he loved for God. No one in his life would be able to compete for God's place.

If we are to experience true worship, our love for God has to supersede our love of anyone and anything else. Jesus set this standard for discipleship, which includes worship.

If any man comes to me, and does

Come, Let Us Worship [*Appreciating the Call to Worship*]

not hate his own father and mother and wife and children and brothers and sisters, yes, even his own life, he cannot be my disciple. (Luke 14:26)

Jesus is not instructing us to hate our families. He makes it clear that the believer must not love anyone, even himself, above God. Abraham's obedience reflects this. Before we enter into His presence with singing, the lifting of hands, and giving of thanks, we have to live a life that constitutes sacrifice and self-denial.

Come, Let Us Worship
[Appreciating the Call to Worship]

Then said Jesus unto his disciples, If any man will come after me, let him deny himself, and take up his cross, and follow me. (Matthew 16:24)

All that will go after Christ have to deny themselves of fleshly and evil desires. The same holds true for worship. If we will go after Him in corporate and personal worship, praise, and prayer, we have to put to death the works of the flesh.

Therefore consider the members of your earthly body as dead to immorality, impurity, passions, evil

Come, Let Us Worship [*Appreciating the Call to Worship*]

desires, and greed, which accounts to idolatry. (Colossians 3:5 NASV)

Paul instructs the believers at Colossae to kill sexual immorality, moral impurity, lust, evil desires, and greediness as followers of Christ. If we hold on to these fleshly attributes, our worship and praise will be ineffective and unacceptable.

Our relationship with Christ demands self-sacrifice. Without it, the depth of worship will be limited. It may also result in rejected worship. All that we give unto God must be pure and undefiled.

Come, Let Us Worship [*Appreciating the Call to Worship*]

I beseech you therefore, brethren, by the mercies of God, that ye present your bodies a living sacrifice, holy, acceptable unto God, which is your reasonable service. And be not conformed to this world: but be ye transformed by the renewing of your mind, that ye may prove what is that good, and acceptable, and perfect, will of God. (Romans 12:1-2)

If we walk in the aforementioned verses, our worship of God will be acceptable, effective, and meaningful. The

Come, Let Us Worship [*Appreciating the Call to Worship*]

work of preparation starts with a mind to give up all to come close to Him. We enter into true worship when we come wholeheartedly and holy.

Our worship is not to be tainted by the world. Again, worship commences with sacrifice, denial, and personal holiness.

Worship is Subsistence

Worship described Abraham's potential sacrifice of Isaac. Further research reveals the depth of his statement. The Hebrew term translated *worship* means to be weighed down. Worship is to be

Come, Let Us Worship [*Appreciating the Call to Worship*]

something that an individual carries consistently.

Abraham's future descendants and God's chosen people were to be weighed down by worship; that is, they were to be worship. The use of this term equated God's people with worship.

This means that the people of God not only engage in worship, but they are worship. From this, we discover that worship is sacrifice *and* subsistence.

<u>Subsistence</u> - the condition of being; condition of managing to stay alive

Come, Let Us Worship [*Appreciating the Call to Worship*]

Worship is Selfless

Worship is to characterize the believer's life and existence. The believer *is* worship. It is to be his condition or state of being. The believer recognizes that it is through the Lord that he exists and does all things.

> *For in him we live, and move, and have our being; as certain also of your own poets have said, For we are also his offspring. (Acts 17:28)*

The believer's life should be a living demonstration of worship. While eating,

Come, Let Us Worship [*Appreciating the Call to Worship*]

sleeping, working, and relaxing, the Lord's glory and honor should not be diminished.

Come, Let Us Worship [*Appreciating the Call to Worship*]

Notes:

_____

_____

_____

_____

_____

_____

_____

_____

Come, Let Us Worship
[Appreciating the Call to Worship]

Come, Let Us Worship [*Appreciating the Call to Worship*]

-Section 2-

O Come, Let Us Worship and Bow Down

-Psalm 95:6

Come, Let Us Worship
[Appreciating the Call to Worship]

Come, Let Us Worship [*Appreciating the Call to Worship*]

What does it mean to worship? In the scriptures, there are numerous meanings to the word we find translated *worship*. When we understand these, we will be able to offer up to God true worship.

O come, let us worship and bow down: let us kneel before the Lord our maker. (Psalm 95:6)

True worship comes from the knowledge that God is Supreme and the Creator of all things. He possesses all wisdom, power, and authority. Worship means to bow down or to prostrate

Come, Let Us Worship [*Appreciating the Call to Worship*]

before His greatness.

Therefore, when we say we worship God, there ought to be some actions that follow. Whether in the religious setting or in the personal lives of believers, worship requires more than a verbal declaration.

When we say that we worship God, we have to demonstrate what we are saying. If not, then our declarations are only empty words. We have to refrain from hypocrisy.

We sing songs and hymns which convey the intent to worship. The only thing

Come, Let Us Worship [*Appreciating the Call to Worship*]

that is lacking is following through. Jesus warned against this type of worship when He exposed the vain worship of the people in His day.

> *This people draweth nigh unto me with their mouth, and honoureth me with their lips; but their heart is far from me. But in vain they do worship me... (Matthew 15:8-9a)*

Our words of worship should never be vain sayings. The words of our mouths should match the intention of our hearts. We have stated that to worship means to

Come, Let Us Worship [*Appreciating the Call to Worship*]

bow down or to prostrate. How does this occur in the religious setting?

When we speak of religious setting, we mean corporate or personal settings set aside for the overall worship and reverence of God.

Again, how is worship to be demonstrated after we have declared our intent through word or song?

Bowing of the Head

Regardless of the setting, when one wants to demonstrate worship, he may bow his head in reverence to God. When the

Come, Let Us Worship [*Appreciating the Call to Worship*]

head is bowed, it symbolizes that our thoughts are turned toward Him.

We submit our ways unto His and our thoughts unto His because God's ways and thoughts are higher than ours.

> *For my thoughts are not your thoughts, neither are your ways my ways, saith the Lord. For as the heavens are higher than the earth, so are my ways higher than your ways, and my thoughts than your thoughts. (Isaiah 55:8-9)*

Come, Let Us Worship [*Appreciating the Call to Worship*]

The bowing of the head demonstrates submission unto God's purposes. It reflects our intention to submit or bow to His wisdom and word. In services, we bow our heads oftentimes when prayers are made. If we do this, we are telling the Lord that we bow our wills to His in response to our requests.

Bowing at the Waist

Depending upon the religious setting, some may feel at liberty to bow unto the Lord while in a standing position (accompanied with the lifting of hands).

Come, Let Us Worship [*Appreciating the Call to Worship*]

This type of bowing demonstrates reverence for His greatness. This type of bowing is done in respect to God as the One who fills heaven and earth.

> *Thus saith the Lord, The heaven is my throne, and the earth is my footstool... (Isaiah 66:1)*

In Asian culture, it is customary to bow when meeting acquaintances and respecting those in authority. In the Church, we are friends and servants of God. We bow to show personal intimacy and respect.

Come, Let Us Worship [*Appreciating the Call to Worship*]

Bowing at the waist also represents that we set our personal desires aside to honor the Lord. This is why usually during corporate worship and personal times of devotion we do not eat, drink, and meet other physical needs to give Him our undivided attention.

Everything we have is to be submitted to Him in the act of worship. It also demonstrates that while we are in worship, we will submit any ungodly desires and appetites of the flesh unto the Lord.

Come, Let Us Worship [*Appreciating the Call to Worship*]

Having therefore these promises, dearly beloved, let us cleanse ourselves from all filthiness of the flesh and spirit, perfecting holiness in the fear of God. (II Corinthians 7:1)

True worship will bring men and women into greater levels of personal holiness. Worship helps us to perfect holiness in the fear of the Lord.

Bending of the Knee(s)

Another common demonstration of worship is to kneel before God. Again, this is oftentimes done in connection to prayer.

Come, Let Us Worship *[Appreciating the Call to Worship]*

When possible, it should be incorporated into the worship setting. Since it involves the legs, kneeling denotes submission to God's ways. It expresses a willingness to go where He wants you to go. Your volition will be governed by His word.

The steps of a good man are ordered by the Lord: and he delighteth in his way. (Psalm 37:23)

When we kneel in the worship setting, we declare God's supremacy. We demonstrate that He alone stands in control of our lives. We submit the course and direction of our lives unto Him. We kneel to demonstrate that He is above us in authority and power.

Prostrating the Body

One of the greatest expressions of worship in the religious setting is prostration. When one prostrates, he/she is on bended knees with the face to the ground or laid out (usually face down) during the time of worship.

This act of worship denotes total surrender the Lord. Prostration reflects a willingness to submit one's total being unto

Come, Let Us Worship [*Appreciating the Call to Worship*]

the Lord. When we do this, we declare our total trust, submission, surrender, and love.

> *Jesus said unto him, Thou shalt love the Lord thy God with all thy heart, and with all thy soul, and with all thy mind. (Matthew 23:27)*

Those that will lay prostrate before Him in worship have to understand that this is what they are communicating. God is in control. No other will be placed before Him. His word is law. His will is unchanging.

Come, Let Us Worship [*Appreciating the Call to Worship*]

If we are going to act this out in the worship setting, then we must be prepared to follow through. If not, we become vain worshippers.

How many times have we sang the song, *"I Surrender All"* in the worship setting? Yet, our lives do not reflect the sentiments of this song.

We do not have to be perfect to sing the words to this song. However, if we are to sing it, we should be striving daily to make it a reality in our lives.

Songs like this should be meaningful

Come, Let Us Worship [*Appreciating the Call to Worship*]

outside of the religious settings. This leads us to the next area of concern. What does worship look in everyday life?

Come, Let Us Worship
[Appreciating the Call to Worship]

Notes:

Come, Let Us Worship
[Appreciating the Call to Worship]

Come, Let Us Worship [*Appreciating the Call to Worship*]

-Section 3-

Worship in Action

Come, Let Us Worship *[Appreciating the Call to Worship]*

Come, Let Us Worship [*Appreciating the Call to Worship*]

In many passages of scriptures, we find the word *worship*. However, the terms used to derive the word *worship* vary in meaning in the original languages.

In this brief section in our study, we will examine the various passages containing worship and their implications for the modern-day worshipper.

Bow/Prostrate to His Standards for Living

O worship the Lord in the beauty of holiness: fear before him, all the earth. (Psalm 69:9)

In this verse, worship means to bow

Come, Let Us Worship [*Appreciating the Call to Worship*]

and prostrate before the Lord. In everyday life, the believer worships God as He submits to His standards for living. We worship God daily when we bow to His commands.

For the grace of God that bringeth salvation hath appeared to all men, Teaching us that, denying ungodliness and worldly lusts, we should live soberly, righteously, and godly, in this present world. (Titus 2:11-12)

Our reception of God's grace teaches

Come, Let Us Worship *[Appreciating the Call to Worship]*

us that true worship manifests in separation and sanctification. When we do this in our lives, we are bowing our lives in worship of Him.

Swim in (Live in) His Presence

Exalt ye the Lord our God, and worship at his footstool; for he is holy. (Psalm 99:5)

The word translated *worship* here means a pond to swim in. The psalmist is calling the people to exalt God and swim in (at) His footstool. We do this when we walk in the Spirit.

Come, Let Us Worship [*Appreciating the Call to Worship*]

If we live in the Spirit, let us also walk in the Spirit. (Galatians 5:25)

Walking by the Spirit constitutes worship. As we allow the Spirit to lead us daily, we worship God. The only way one is able to swim is there

is an abundance of water.

As we are filled daily with the Holy Spirit and submit to His unction, we are in worship.

Serve the Lord in Ministry and Good Works

But this I confess unto thee, that after

Come, Let Us Worship [*Appreciating the Call to Worship*]

the way which they call heresy, so worship I the God of my fathers, believing all things which are written in the law and in the prophets. (Acts 24:14)

In his defense of the gospel, Paul stated that he worshipped the God of Israel. The word he used for worship denoted religious service. He described worship of God by faithfully ministering and serving for Him and in His name.

Thus, we worship God as we witness in His name and perform good works, which

Come, Let Us Worship *[Appreciating the Call to Worship]*

includes organized religious service.

Let your light so shine before men, that they may see your good works, and glorify your Father, which is in heaven. (Matthew 5:16)

God receives glory when we perform good works. Good works are an outward of an inner relationship. When they are done with the right motives, we worship God through them. When we serve in the Church, do volunteer work, and the like, we worship God through our actions.

Come, Let Us Worship [*Appreciating the Call to Worship*]

True worship will come from reverence and awe of God's authority, majesty, and greatness. Worship sets God on the throne and places us at His feet. When we walk in worship, we walk in the fear of the Lord. Our fear is born out of respect for who He is. His supremacy is seen and felt throughout all creation.

Serve the Lord with fear, and rejoice with trembling. (Psalm 2:11)

If one does not respect, fear, and reverence God, the worship offered is a religious exercise only. Worship that is

Come, Let Us Worship [*Appreciating the Call to Worship*]

acceptable unto God transcends the religious setting and permeates through everyday living. When we offer this type of worship, God is exalted and we will be transformed in His presence (in or outside of the church setting).

Come, Let Us Worship
[Appreciating the Call to Worship]

Notes:

Come, Let Us Worship
[Appreciating the Call to Worship]

Come, Let Us Worship [*Appreciating the Call to Worship*]

Glossary of Terms

PRAISE: sing a hymn, celebrate, group celebration, commend

WORSHIP: Israelite, prostrate, bow, to swim in, prostrate, to serve, minister to God, revere and adore

MAGNIFY: to heap up (like sheaves)

EXALT: to mount up, rise, to heave

Come, Let Us Worship [*Appreciating the Call to Worship*]

Glossary of Terms

EXTOL: hold out, extended hands, throw a stone

GLADNESS: remission (of debt) or suspension of labor

BLESS: kneel in reverence, salute, extinguish, to speak well of

GLORIFY: promote, honor, respect, rest, prepare an habitation, boast, esteem, glorious, to thirst for

Come, Let Us Worship [*Appreciating the Call to Worship*]

Notes:

Come, Let Us Worship
[Appreciating the Call to Worship]

Come, Let Us Worship [*Appreciating the Call to Worship*]

Bibliography

Lockman Foundation. *Comparative Study Bible.* Zondervan Publishing House. Grand Rapids, MI, c1984

The Bible Library. *The Bible Library CD Rom Disc.* Ellis Enterprises Incorporated, (c) 1988 – 2000. 4205 McAuley Blvd., Suite 385, Oklahoma City, OK 73120. All Rights Reserved.

Come, Let Us Worship [*Appreciating the Call to Worship*]

Encarta® World English Dictionary [North American Edition] © & (P) 2006 Microsoft Corporation. All Rights Reserved. Developed for Microsoft by Bloomsbury Publishing Plc.

Come, Let Us Worship

[Appreciating the Call to Worship]

Notes:

_____

_____

_____

_____

_____

_____

_____

_____

_____

Come, Let Us Worship
[Appreciating the Call to Worship]

Come, Let Us Worship
[Appreciating the Call to Worship]

Come, Let Us Worship [*Appreciating the Call to Worship*]

Come, Let Us Worship

[Appreciating the Call to Worship]

Come, Let Us Worship *[Appreciating the Call to Worship]*

Come, Let Us Worship

[Appreciating the Call to Worship]

Come, Let Us Worship *[Appreciating the Call to Worship]*

www.ingramcontent.com/pod-product-compliance
Lightning Source LLC
Chambersburg PA
CBHW050343010526
44119CB00049B/683